Entrepreneur Mindset Series

TOP HABITS OF SUCCESSFUL ENTREPRENEURS

Steve Jobs, Bill Gates, Jeff Bezos, Elon Musk, Arianna
Huffington, Warren Buffett, and Richard Branson

*

A. J. PARR

*

GRAPEVINE BOOKS

FIRST EDITION 2020

Copyright © 2020 A. J. Parr. All Rights Reserved

ALL RIGHTS RESERVED – FAIR USE

ALL RIGHTS RESERVED under Title 17, U.S. Code, International, and Pan-American Copyright Conventions. The sharing, duplication, distribution, uploading, or transfer of this electronic book by any digital or printed means without the explicit permission of the publisher is unauthorized.

DISCLAIMER: The 1976 Copyright Act (Section 107) states that "fair use" is permitted when writing criticism, comments, news reports, and didactic texts (otherwise infringing). Non-profit, educational, or personal use favor fair use. Napoleon Hill quotes taken from the 1937 edition of "Think and Grow Rich" presently in the Public Domain

AUTHOR: A.J. Parr

PUBLISHED BY: Grapevine Books.

Copyright © 2020 A. J. Parr. All Rights Reserved.

ISBN: 9798684187513

C O N T E N T

ABOUT THIS BOOK

"Good habits are hard to develop but easy to live with; bad habits are easy to develop but hard to live with. The habits you have and the habits that have you will determine almost everything you achieve or fail to achieve."

Brian Tracy

What do Jeff Bezos, Steve Jobs, Elon Musk, Sir Richard Branson, Bill Gates, Warren Buffett, and Arianna Huffington all have in common? Of course, they all managed to follow their dreams regardless of just how many times they had to face failure and became wealthy and successful entrepreneurs. But that's not all they have in common.

First and foremost, they embodied the *Top Habits of Successful Entrepreneurs*, which are available for everyone, including you.

When it comes to winning, some entrepreneurs are smarter, more talented, or have more resources, which allows them to stay a cut above the rest. However, as evidenced in this book, there is a set of specific habits that makes the difference if you want to succeed—and I mean really succeed!

Most people have some of these habits, but the trick is to embody them all. In any case, no matter what stage of the "game" you're in, my advice is to read these pages, apply its teachings and get ready for the success you deserve.

WHY I WROTE THIS BOOK

Around 20 years ago, I first read the inspirational book *"Think and Grow Rich,"* written by the American reporter Napoleon Hill after interviewing over 500 self-made millionaires over 20 years. As Hill concluded, *"both success and failure are largely the results of HABIT!"*

Back then, I was stuck in the corporate world, working 40+ hours a week with no other known way to make a living. I had a family to feed and did not want to give up the security of my day job nor my regular paycheck in exchange for financial freedom.

I spent the next few years trying out different business ideas in my spare time. But, one by one, they all flopped. Of course, I also spent a great deal of time getting over my failures and rebuilding enough confidence to give it another try.

All I knew was that I was not willing to give up trying. I would not quit that easily. So, I continued reading all I could on entrepreneurship, financial education, business management, spirituality, and, especially, on the lives of the world's top entrepreneurs of all times.

Finally, almost ten years ago, I put everything I had learned into practice, left my day job, and started a successful online business that gradually grew. Since then, I've been working from the comfort of my home, living a pleasant, peaceful life with my family, and enjoying the financial independence and stability that only self-employment brings.

Perhaps the most important lesson I have learned during these decades is that our habits determine our success, as the American inspirational author Og Mandino pointed out in his runaway bestseller, *"The Greatest Salesman in The World"*:

"In truth, the only difference between those who have failed and those who have succeeded lies in the difference of their habits. Good habits are the key to all success. Bad habits are the unlocked door to failure."

I now write this book with the object of sharing my experience and explaining how success depends more on our habits than on factors like intelligence, talent, resources, expertise, education, social background, or even business skills. Not even being too young seems to play a vital role anymore, as evidenced by the increasing number of teens who have made their first million dollars before reaching the age of 20.

My conclusion is that in business, as well as in sports, habits determine who wins or not, as stated by the American NFL executive and football coach Vincent Lombardi:

"Winning is a habit. Unfortunately, so is losing."

UNDERSTANDING HUMAN HABITS

According to the Encyclopaedia Britannica, a habit is *"any regularly repeated behavior that requires little or no thought and is learned rather than innate."* In essence, habits are learned behaviors that are repetitive and automatic. For instance, if you instinctively put your seatbelt on before starting your car or reach for a cigarette each time you drink coffee, it means you have a habit.

Some habits are good for us—like washing our hands before eating or looking both ways before crossing the street. But others can be rather nasty—like chain-smoking or nail-biting—and can also be very hard to stop.

Both knowingly and unknowingly, our habits determine most of what we do in our daily lives. They can be as simple as brushing our teeth, driving to work, or setting out our working schedule for the day. Research has shown that most of these activities are not conscious, but only repetitive actions we perform unconsciously, as though in "auto-pilot."

In any case, habits can either make us or break us. As repetitive, unconscious actions, they determine both our thoughts and our behavior, ultimately influencing our aspirations in life as well as our daily living.

Perhaps you are an experienced entrepreneur who is facing hard times and don't know what to do. Or maybe you presently have a steady job and dream with calling it quits, or are struggling with unemployment and seek to be self-employed. In any case, this book is for you.

In the following pages, I will share most of what I learned about the *Top Habits of Successful Entrepreneurs* and how these shaped the lives of prosperous people like Steve Jobs, Elon Musk, Jeff Bezos, Bill Gates, Ariana Huffington, Warren Buffett, Oprah Winfrey, and Sir Richard Branson, among others. My wish is to help you learn about these essential habits and achieve your highest goal.

Now, tell me, are you ready to take action and leave the passenger seat of your life for good?

1.-THE HABIT OF PURSUING LIFE GOALS

"If we think long term, we can accomplish things that we couldn't otherwise accomplish."

Jeff Bezos.

I f you seek success and financial freedom but are presently caught up in the busyness of life, working from 9 to 5 or stuck in a regressive cycle of repeating the same mistakes over and over again, then this book is for you.

Its pages will help you analyze your habits, detect the least desirable, and replace them with those that have played a vital role in the lives of some of the world's most successful entrepreneurs.

To begin, let us also analyze the worst and most common habit of unsuccessful people: the habit of going through life without a real purpose or goal, as Napoleon Hill describes in *"Think and Grow Rich"*:

"There are fifteen major causes of failure that I have discovered... The first one is the habit of drifting through life without a definite purpose or a definite plan for attaining it. You may be surprised that ninety-eight out of every hundred people belong in that category, as drifters. They're like goldfish in a bowl: they go round and round, always coming back to the starting point, but never getting anywhere.

"The reason they don't get anywhere is, first of all, they don't discover this marvelous gift of the mind, which is capable of determining their earthly destiny. Second, if they do discover it, they don't make proper use of it. Drifting. Lacking in singleness of purpose. Lacking a plan for carrying out the purpose. There you have the major reason for all failures in this world."

It must be noted that most of the world's self-made billionaires admit having a primary purpose or goal in life other than just making money. And this seems to make the difference and sets them apart.

For example, Steve Jobs, the co-founder of Apple computers and CEO of Pixar and NeXT, whose impact on

8

the world continues today thanks to his many accomplishments in technology, product development, and innovation, used to say that our long-term goals grant us purpose and direction in life. In contrast, our short-term goals make us stay on track.

He founded Apple at the age of 21, and within four years, due to the wide success of the high-tech products he helped to develop, his net worth was 217 million dollars!

His priority in life was to contribute to the world in the most significant way possible and to build *"an enduring company that prioritized people,"* as stated by his biographer Walter Isaacson: *"Everything else – products and profits – while still important, would be secondary."*

For the British entrepreneur, investor, and philanthropist Sir Richard Branson, *"there is no greater thing you can do with your life and your work than follow your passions in a way that serves the world and you."*

Regarding his life mission, he admits:

"I have always been driven by the desire to change things for the better. That was what motivated my friends and me to launch our first business, "Student Magazine," in the 1960s. We wanted to give young people a voice on issues such as the Vietnam War.

That spirit of hopefulness and commitment to concrete change continued through every business we launched afterward, and it's still true for our newer businesses like Virgin Galactic, the world's first commercial space company."

On the other hand, the South African engineer and technology expert Elon Musk, founder of PayPal and CEO of Tesla, recently said he founded his aerospace company SpaceX to save the human race from extinction, making sure that we, as a species, are assured of the best chance to survive in the future. Now, that's what I call a colossal goal!

And you? Do you have a life dream that you would like to make come true? What is it, exactly? Are you actively working on it or not doing anything about it? And do you believe you can materialize it, or are you convinced it will never come true?

The American entrepreneur and motivational speaker Tony Robbins, who manages over 50 businesses that gross around $6 billion in annual sales, recommends having a broad vision, plus an achievable plan. He also stresses that the purpose of any goal *"is not to get it, but who you become in pursuit of it."* If chasing your life dream makes you grow, then you have achieved success.

To determine your highest goal in life, try to find that which most inspires and motivates you, your biggest passion, your most outstanding talent.

Regarding the importance of having a special mission in life, the Chicago animator, entrepreneur, and film producer Walt Disney recommended setting goals capable of transcending time:

"Think beyond your lifetime if you want to accomplish something truly worthwhile... *A person should set his goals as early as he can and devote all his energy and talent to getting there. With enough effort, he may achieve it. Or he may find something that is even more rewarding. But in the end, no matter what the outcome, he will know he has been alive."*

Without a specific goal or significant purpose in life, it's hard to attract the things you most desire.

The innovative Internet entrepreneur Jeff Bezos followed his dream when he launched Amazon.com as an online bookstore back in 1995. Although it started out of his garage, and he warned his investors that there was a 70% chance his venture would fail or go bankrupt, his long-term vision was to transform it into *"an everything store."* Today, when Amazon holds the title **as the world's largest online retailer**

and Bezos has become the richest man in the world, he admits:

"I would always encourage people to hold, powerfully, to a vision and be so stubborn of it. Don't let anybody move you off of your vision."

Regarding *Blue Origin*, Bezos' aerospace manufacturer and sub-orbital spaceflight company, his amazing long-term goal is to create *"the infrastructure for millions of people to live and work in space."*

YOUR "DEFINITE CHIEF AIM"

In *"Think and Grow Rich,"* Napoleon Hill recommends writing down your primary future goal or *"Definite Chief Aim,"* including the exact amount of money you want to receive as well as what you intend to give in return, plus a definite date when you plan to accomplish this.

Once you have outlined your plan, he suggests putting it into action at once, whether you are ready or not. He also recommends reading your written statement aloud, twice a day, once when you rise in the morning and the other just before retiring at night.

Following this advice, in 1969, the Hong Kong American actor and martial arts expert Bruce Lee wrote down his *"Definite Chief Aim"* as follows:

I, Bruce Lee, will be the first highest paid Oriental superstar in the United States. In return, I will give the most exciting performances and render the best of quality in the capacity of an actor. Starting 1970, I will achieve world fame, and from then onward, till the end of 1980, I will have in my possession $10,000,000. I will live the way I please and achieve inner harmony and happiness.

Bruce Lee, Jan. 1969

Although Lee died scarcely four years later from brain edema, he managed to become a famous movie star in Asia and, posthumously, in America. The year he died, his fortune was around $10 million.

One month after his death, Warner Bros. released in the US Lee's last film, *"Enter the Dragon,"* which became a box-office hit, eventually grossing more than $200 million and turning Lee into a superstar in America, as he had planned.

SECRET

My Definite Chief Aim

I, Bruce Lee, will be the first highest paid Oriental super Star in the United States. In return I will give the most exciting performances and render the best of quality in the capacity of an actor. Starting 1970 I will achieve world fame and from then onward till the end of 1980 I will have in my possession $10,000,000. I will live the way I please and achieve inner harmony and happiness

Bruce Lee

Jan. 1969

SECRET

2.-THE HABIT OF RISK-TAKING

"The riskiest moment for Amazon was at the very, very beginning... That was 1995, and the first question every investor asked me was: 'What's the Internet?'"

Jeff Bezos

Taking risks is part of being a successful entrepreneur. Now, this might sound counterintuitive and make some people uneasy. But it is increasingly essential if you seek to succeed.

You must be thinking, *"I want to reach success, and for that, I need a well-thought-out life plan and plenty of stability. I do not want to be taking risks and expose myself to possible loss and failure. Why would I do that?"* Well, the reality is quite different than what many may think. Life is unpredictable; it is full of tangibles and intangibles. But the truth of the matter is that real winners have to be willing to take risks, test their limits, be adaptive, and overcome their fears!

Some of today's most outstanding companies would never have succeeded had their founders not taken enormous risks. Google, Apple, Microsoft, Tesla, Whole Foods Market, The Huffington Post, Virgin Atlantic Airways, Flickr, Oracle, and Netflix were all considered financial risks with low chances of survival when they started. And the list goes on...

MAKING A DREAM COME TRUE

In 1993, the 29-year-old senior vice president of the New York investment fund D. E. Shaw & Company, decided to give up his salary of over $1 million a year to follow a dream. All because he and his boss had made an important discovery while researching the Internet: Web usage was growing at a fantastic rate of 2,300 percent per year! He knew that anything growing that fast was worth looking into. And so, after analyzing several possibilities, the young vice-president decided to take the biggest risk of his life and left his high-paying job to start an online venture, something in which he had no experience at all!

We all know what happened next: The young man drove from New York to Seattle, rented a small house in a suburb, got the support of a few investors, and started an online bookstore in his garage. And thus, initially known as Cadabra, Amazon.com was born!

Of course, Jeff Bezos was a true visionary and risk-taker. And it paid him off. Since then, he has taken many other great gambles, some for better and some for worse. But that's what real leaders do, is it not?

Today, that same high-risk mentality is crucial to Amazon's strategy, as Bezos points out:

"As a company grows, everything needs to scale, including the size of your failed experiments. If the size of your failures isn't growing, you're not going to be inventing at a size that can actually move the needle."

Taking risks does not always imply you will succeed. And this is perfectly normal. Of course, it is usually uncomfortable and generates uncertainty. However, when leaders push the boundaries and conquer their dreams, they not only open the doors for their own progress, but also encourage others to stretch and take risks, too.

IMPORTANCE OF CONFRONTING YOUR FEARS

When you take risks, your thoughts will probably be clouded with personal fears: *"What if I lose all my money? What if I become a laughing stock in front of everyone?"* All these fears constrict you from truly making the most of your abilities. And they are mostly irrational because our brain usually goes into a frenzy every time we step out of our comfort zones. However, taking risks helps you confront your fears and eventually get over them, allowing you to tackle your vulnerability and become stronger.

You will only fear it until you do it.

The idea of leaving a million-dollar job to start an uncertain online venture was completely outrageous until Jeff Bezos turned his dream into reality. Think of how much fear and hesitation must have gone into that project. But Bezos was willing to take the needed risks.

The creation of his aerospace company Blue Origin is another example of how Bezos took a critical leap of faith, but he was not afraid to push the boundaries.

Many believed he would fail, but Bezos never let that taint his ambition, and today, his enterprises are soaring more than ever!

A WORLD OF NEW POSSIBILITIES

You will never know what lays outside, in the cold open, until you venture into it. Your fears and self-doubts might hold you back, but once you overcome them and take this risk by putting yourself on the line, you can create an entirely different set of opportunities and possibilities for yourself.

Perhaps you have been successful in achieving your initial goal and have found other things that fuel your interest more. Maybe it is time to take new risks and discover new ways to grow and improve. In any case, you will never know your full potential unless you try. So, keep an open mind, and take risks even when the odds don't seem to be in your favor.

Here's the thing with taking business risks, no matter how absurd or crazy they may sound, you can only gain by taking them! Of course, if you take a risk, there is always a chance of failing. In any case, assuming it will help you develop a whole different set of skills and recognize what works and what doesn't.

Mistakes can show you what not to do and also boost your insight and experience. So, what's the harm? In any case, whether you win or lose, it will help you grow and learn.

INACTIVITY: THE RECIPE TO FAILURE

If you spend the rest of your life barricaded behind walls you have created by underestimating your capabilities, living within the box of your own fears and insecurities, you will never be successful in business.

You cannot live forever facing inaction. How can someone who is stagnant succeed in life? If you do nothing, then obviously nothing will ever happen. You need to get off that couch, take risks, and make your move!

Regarding the importance of leaving your comfort zone and overcoming your fears, the American talk show host, television producer, and entrepreneur Oprah Winfrey says:

"I believe that one of life's greatest risks is never daring to risk."

Therefore, my advice is to start taking risks today. Right now. Yes, now!

Have faith in yourself, just like Jeff Bezos and countless others who have taken significant risks to succeed in life have done. Try things you have never done before. Change your whole strategy towards something new. Start questioning your own limits and bounds. Do unthinkable things. Prepare yourself as best as you can. Assess each risk carefully. And, in the end, you will find that there is nothing to lose as long as you are willing to learn from your failures.

3.-THE HABIT OF POSITIVE THINKING

"You want to have a future where you're expecting things to be better, not one where you're expecting things to be worse."

Elon Musk

E lon Musk entered the Internet frenzy in 1995 with a company called Zip2—which he sold for $22 million. He then concentrated on his next online venture, which evolved into PayPal—of which he was the largest shareholder when eBay bought it for $1.5 billion. Today, as head of the booming high-tech companies Tesla and SpaceX, and with a net worth of $70.5 billion (surpassing Buffett), he admits the importance of always expecting the best:

"If you wake up in the morning and think the future is going to be better, it is a bright day. Otherwise, it's not."

Yes, we've all heard it before. We are what we think. What we believe we can achieve. Everything depends on the color of the crystal through which we see. We have all heard these maxims, repeated from time and time again by all sorts of people. But it's true. Whether you see the glass half-full or half-empty, is entirely up to you and your thinking habits.

If you are someone who is continually thinking about negative things, faults and flaws of both yourself and others, diminishing your self-esteem, overthinking everything, taunting yourself, holding grudges and regrets, comparing your situation with others, blaming exterior things for the issues in your life, then you have the habit of negative thinking. And, unless you do something about it, sooner or later, this habit will trigger the downfall of your entrepreneurial career.

Indeed, we all become what we think.

A POSITIVE MENTAL ATTITUDE

When you perform certain activities or deem certain things, your brain releases certain chemicals. One such chemical is called cortisol, which is a happy hormone. When our brain secretes cortisol, we feel energized and content. And, when you are content and happy with yourself, you start to have a productive mindset. You start to believe that anything is possible. You make huge strides and get massive projects done and dusted. You are motivated, and it becomes easier for you to tackle complicated tasks. This cortisol boost triggers positive thinking, a positive attitude, as well as the development of positive habits.

Your habits, both positive and negative, are interlinked with your thinking patterns. If you think positively, you will see a brighter world and attract positive energy around you. Optimistic and productive people will step into your life. You will be more proactive, and thus, you will progress in life. All this will boost your inner energy and nourish your brain.

Positive thinking supports the healthy well-being of your body and mind and minimizes negative influences such as stress, depression, regrets, and remorse.

Whereas, on the contrary, if your brain becomes prone to thinking negatively, taking into account only the cons of a particular situation or person, you will start going downhill. Toxic energy will flood your brain, and stress and depression will become your only mates.

Life has its problems. And our job is to deal with them the best way we can. Negative thinking only makes matters worse.

Remember, you are what you think. It all begins with the way you think. This is why you need to maintain a positive mindset, especially in the face of hardships and complications. In times of trouble, do not allow the dark forces of your mind to claim victory. Otherwise, you will simply fail.

So how can you maintain a positive mental attitude?

Let's take a look at a few ways:

1.-Always believe in yourself and your life goal

In times when everything seems to be lost, focus on believing in yourself and your life goal. In all cases, keep a positive mental attitude, as Tony Robbins recommends:

"The power of positive thinking is the ability to generate a feeling of certainty in yourself when nothing in the environment supports you."

The American scientist and inventor Thomas Alva Edison, creator of the phonograph, the kinetoscope, the Dictaphone, the autographic printer, the carbon microphone, and the electric lamp or incandescent light bulb, was a great believer in positive thinking. He was almost entirely deaf, but this did not bother him. On the contrary, as Neil Baldwin, one of his biographers claims: *"This condition made him feel like he could think more and he could concentrate more. He became very introspective. He often felt like he was alone even when there were other people around."*

In 1914, when a massive fire burned down Edison's lab complex in New Jersey, destroying almost his entire operation, The New York Times sent a reporter to the scene of the blaze, who quoted him as saying:

"Although I am over 67 years old, I'll start all over again tomorrow."

Another case worth mentioning involves an aspiring young cartoonist who back in 1919, scarcely five years after Edison's lab burned down, was fired from his job at a Kansas City newspaper. He couldn't believe it when his editor said his cartoons simply weren't good enough! But, instead of calling it quits and changing his line of work, the cartoonist continued believing in himself and his higher purpose in life, turned to the power of positive thinking, and eventually gave humanity the wonderful world of Walt Disney!

2.-Focus on Solutions, not on Problems

Positive thinking is a way of life. Only you can decide what affects you and what consumes your mind.

If you choose to focus on the problems in your life, you start to develop a victim mentality and end up thinking of how life always keeps thrashing you with endless burdens and difficulties, and how you will never get out of this negative cycle. You also start to think less of yourself, your confidence starts to plummet, and your energy ends up dropping down.

The lives of the most successful entrepreneurs teach us that whenever we are hit with a bump in the road, we must not dwell on how mammoth the problem is. Instead of this, develop the task of breaking the task down. Divide it into smaller, more doable chunks. This will stimulate your brain to start focusing on the solutions.

It all starts with your mind. So, if you catch yourself thinking about how problem-ridden your life is, think about how you can work on those problems. Think big, don't let your troubles bring you down. As we will see, every problem, as well as every failure, holds the seed of future success.

3.-Beware of your self-talk

We all have an inner voice, and the way we dialogue with it defines our relationship with ourselves and influences our thinking process.

Therefore, whenever you communicate with yourself, be careful with the choice of your words. Instead of saying, *"I can't do this or that,"* say, *"I can do this, and I will!"*

The words *"no, not, never, and cannot"* should not be part of your vocabulary.

4.-Celebrate small victories

When was the last time you praised yourself over something seemingly small? You should always celebrate small accomplishments, for they pave the path to more significant achievements, as the Hollywood superstar and entrepreneur Arnold Schwarzenegger recommends:

"Look for small victories and build on that. Each small victory, even if it is just getting up five minutes earlier, gives you confidence. You realize that these little victories make you feel great, and you keep going. You realize that being paralyzed by fear of failure is worse than failure."

4.-Begin the day on a positive note:

Wake up, look in the mirror, and take pride in who you are. Starting your day on a positive note determines your entire outlook on the day. It builds your self-esteem and confidence. You feel surer of yourself. You feel stronger, more invincible with every foot you put down.

Remember what Elon Musk says: If you start the day thinking it will be a great day, then it most probably will!

5.-Practice Gratitude:

Gratitude is a powerful tool. Expressing gratitude and being grateful for all your blessings will help you maintain a positive mindset. Gratitude also makes you sensitive to the suffering of others and allows you to give back to the community, to the people who might not be as privileged as you may be. This helps to keep you grounded.

Arianna Huffington, the founder of *The Huffington Post* and *Thrive Global*, believes that it is not happy people who are thankful but grateful people who are happy. She works gratitude into her life by habit stacking, which is a simple method of adding meaning to the mundane moments of our day by practicing gratitude in those moments.

A. J. Parr

4.-THE HABIT OF CONTINUOUS LEARNING

"I love the challenge of learning about industries I know nothing about."

Sir Richard Branson

Sir Richard Branson, the founder of the Virgin Group, which controls over 400 companies in various fields and over 30 countries, once expressed:

"Leaders should be visible, accessible, and approachable, and never stop learning."

That's precisely what most self-made billionaires do. They take time to study the trends, stay up to date on what's current, learn new skills and become experts in different fields.

The American entrepreneur and industrialist Henry Ford, founder of the Ford Motor Company, used to say:

"Anyone who stops learning is old, whether they are twenty or eighty."

And he was right. Life is all about learning. And, to succeed in business, you must keep up with a world that is continuously changing. As you know, there are new inventions, modifications, and technologies being introduced all the time. Every field, be it computer science or communications, is advancing and progressing at lights speed.

One theory or law, which was treated as a fact yesterday, might be proven false today. Besides, if you want to thrive in this world, you need to stay updated with the lingo. Otherwise, someone with a better algorithm will come and throw you off your high horse. Therefore, always be in a constant search to improve, to be better, and to be more successful.

To make a real difference in the business world, you need to regularly and actively increase your general and specific knowledge. In fact, learning must never stop, for it not only helps you to grow your mental capacity but also helps you develop your business or start-ups in new, unforeseen ways.

If Steve Jobs, after developing the first iPhone prototype, would not have tirelessly worked on it to make it more advanced, accessible and easier to use, he would have never achieved the same level of success that he did because some other competitor would have surpassed his invention.

So how do you ingrain this habit of continuous growth and learning in your life?

1.-Develop the habit of reading

One of the most important habits you can develop is the habit of reading, which also includes listening to audiobooks.

Microsoft founder Bill Gates, who admits reading about 50 books a year, considers reading *"absolutely"* essential to success:

"You don't really start getting old until you stop learning... Every book teaches me something new or helps me see things differently. I was lucky to have

parents who encouraged me to read. Reading fuels a sense of curiosity about the world, which I think helped drive me forward in my career and in the work that I do now with my foundation."

The American investor, and business tycoon Warren Buffett, who also highlights the importance of this activity, admits spending most of the day reading newspapers and financial reports, and says his knowledge stacks up *"like compound interest."*

Oprah Winfrey, who is also an avid reader, admits that books are *"her personal path to freedom,"* while Facebook CEO Mark Zuckerberg considers that *"books allow you to fully explore a topic and immerse yourself in a deeper way than most media today."*

2.-Challenge your methodology:

One of the consequences of adopting a strict working routine that is, going through issues and things in a set way is that you may end up becoming stubborn. Then, if a new, unknown obstacle comes your way, you probably won't be able to deal with it. Not if it requires you to adopt a completely different strategy.

This is why, every now and then, you need to rev things up. Change your way of doing things. Adopt a different pattern, a different methodology. Try a new deft technique or process. Apply a new principle. You might end up finding something more proficient, paving the way for your success.

Remember, when Steve Jobs was kicked out of Apple, he had to reinvent himself and work on an entirely different business. This capability allowed him to lead Pixar Animation Studios to success with the production of the first fully-digital animated movie *"Toy Story."* As a matter of fact, it was Pixar and not Apple which made him his first billion dollars.

If Jobs had been apprehensive of change and unfit to adapt to the new circumstances that challenged his previous methodology, Pixar would have never triumphed. But, instead of this, he opted to continue learning and growing, and this led him to succeed.

3.-Never think you know it all.

There are many vital habits that differentiate successful people from ultra-successful people, millionaires from billionaires, legends from icons. One of these is the habit of always thinking you know everything. You can never have the most definite and accurate knowledge on a topic at any given time. There will always be someone who knows a little more about it than you do. On the other hand, perhaps they do not know more about it than you do, but they are aware of something that you are not particularly aware of.

Therefore, wherever you are, whoever you are with, whatever post or accolades you hold, never stop learning from those who are inferior to you as well as those who are superior. Make conversation with them. Learn from them. Even if they have nothing of substance to say, they may have a personality trait that you could pick up on.

Find a mentor in every setting. Try to learn something from everyone. Never stop looking for opportunities to learn new things. Try something you have never done before. Embrace change and innovations with an open mindset.

If, at any point in time, you feel as if you are not learning from the current group of people you have bonded with, then *"change your room."* As Lorne Michaels once said, *"If you're the smartest person in the room, you're in the wrong room."*

A wrong room is a room where you do not gain anything; you hit a flat line, a constant stage in the graph, albeit to be successful in life, you need to have a continually increasing gradient to ensure a proper learning curve.

5.-THE HABIT OF BEING PROACTIVE

"Doing the best at this moment puts you in the best place for the next moment."

Oprah Winfrey

Oprah Gail Winfrey was born into poverty in rural Mississippi to a teenage single mother who left her in the care of her maternal grandmother. As she later admitted, she was continuously molested during her childhood and early teens. At 14, she became pregnant, but her son was born prematurely and died in his infancy.

"I was beaten regularly," she told David Letterman during a lecture series at Ball State University. However, these problems, among others she suffered during her youth and early adulthood, built her strong character and proactive personality. As she told Letterman, *"My story just helped define and shape me as does everybody's story... I am so grateful for my years literally living in poverty because it makes the experience of creating success and building success that much more rewarding..."*

As a result of her troubled past, in fact, Oprah developed a number of character traits that eventually allowed her to succeed as a talk-show host, for she was able to connect with her guests and the public better than anyone. It also turned her into a proactive person during her professional career, from deciding to become a news journalist, to owning her own television show, to creating a magazine, to starting a television network.

Like other proactive individuals, she not only chooses just how to get things done but also how to react or adjust when things go wrong.

WHEN OPPORTUNITY KNOCKS AT YOUR DOOR

One characteristic of proactive individuals is they always know when to take advantage of unexpected opportunities, even when they are not ready for them.

Such is the case of Sir Richard Branson, who recommends that *"if somebody offers you an amazing opportunity, but you are not sure you can do it, say yes, then learn how to do it later."*

Branson followed his own advice when he conceived the idea of creating his successful airline Virgin Atlantic under adverse circumstances, to which he reacted by proactively coming up with a profitable solution, as we shall now see.

It all started at Beef Island (part of the Virgin Islands), where he and his wife had been vacationing. They were waiting for a plane at the international airport when their local flight to Puerto Rico got canceled. Unexpectedly, they had been stranded there with the rest of the passengers, and without another flight scheduled for that day. Most people would have taken this as a 'problem' and feel frustrated or angry. But not Branson, whose millionaire mindset saw this as a challenging opportunity.

Almost at once, he called a few aircraft charter companies and hired a private plane for $2,000. Knowing that other passengers were also stranded, he borrowed a blackboard, wrote *"Virgin Airways $39 Single Flight to Puerto Rico,"* and an hour later, all the seats had been sold out!

This left him thinking, especially after one of the passengers said: *"Virgin Airways isn't too bad. Smarten up the service a little, and you could be in business."* It must be noted that up to then, Branson had never thought about creating an airline. But being as proactive as he is, he worked on his idea, ended up launching Virgin Atlantic, and the rest is aeronautical history!

The amazing thing about Branson was that he did not use any of his money to solve his *"problem."* He used his millionaire mindset and thinking to turn a problem into an opportunity, which not only solved his problem but made him even more money.

So, if you are not creating tremendous wealth right now, it is because you are not taking the right actions. In other words, if you want to massively change the results in your life, you have to take different actions. To take different actions, you have to think differently.

And of course, to think differently, you must adopt a different mindset... a more proactive mindset!

THE TRAIT OF PROACTIVITY

A proactive person is someone who is continuously hustling, not to react to things but to solve those things. Being proactive can cause your life to flip a full 180 degrees.

First of all, you need to know that you have to develop the habit of being proactive if you aspire to succeed. So, don't be a dead fish and go with a flow. Take action and react to changing circumstances. Only you can take charge of your life, so embrace the driving seat of your life now. But only if you have full authority of your life choices, your decisions, actions, inactions, etc.

Remember: Nothing is going to happen unless you make it happen. You are the only person in control of your success and your failures. Your partners, your family, your friends are there to support you, but they cannot take action on your behalf. You are the only real owner of your problems, flaws, and faults. So, solve them on your own, because no one is going to do it for you.

When faced with an issue, there are only so many ways to go about it. Either you blame it on others, complain about it, and try not to face it, or you can actively work to find a solution to it.

Sure, we all run into problems, but what sets us apart is how we solve them. Don't let your faulty past affect you. Whatever happened has happened. You cannot control it now, but you can control what happens from here on. The outcome is at your discretion.

ALWAYS HOLD YOURSELF ACCOUNTABLE

Perhaps one of the most toxic traits is blaming your problems on others or throwing your tasks onto others. Remember that you cannot keep having others do your work for you, a point will come where you will have to deal with it.

Not everyone has the same circumstances. What truly counts is what you make of them. If you aren't consistent in your efforts to improve, to learn, to prepare yourself, then pursuing entrepreneurial success is pointless.

You don't have to be perfect in what you do, but at least you have to be consistent. You also need to make conscious efforts to keep with your habits; otherwise, these habits will not be woven into the fabric of your mind, and you will go back to being the way you were. Only consistency will allow you to leave a footprint on this world.

A. J. Parr

6.-THE HABIT OF MANAGING TIME

"The rich invest in time; the poor invest in money."

Warren Buffett

With almost 70 billion dollars to his name, Warren Buffett is consistently ranked among the wealthiest entrepreneurs in the world, occupying the sixth place on the Bloomberg Billionaires Index (dominated by Jeff Bezos, Bill Gates, Mark Zuckerberg, Elon Musk, and Bernard Arnault).

Despite his immense wealth and the fact that he can buy practically anything he wants (and much more than nearly everyone else could ever dream of), there is something he definitely cannot buy, and that is time.

According to Buffett, the only thing we can do is to make the best use of the time we have. And that's why he recommends saying no to what's least important:

"The difference between successful people and very successful people is that very successful people say 'no' to almost everything."

Worth mentioning is a famous conversation he had with his private airplane pilot, Mike Flint, who needed some advice.

Flint mentioned how the fact of having so many different career priorities and so little time made it increasingly difficult for him to decide what to do.

Buffett silently listened to him, and when he finished, he asked the pilot to do a simple 3-step exercise that would certainly help him straighten out his mind and allow him to make the best choice.

STEP1:

First, Buffett asked Flint to write down his top 25 career goals, which he did after thinking about it for some minutes.

STEP 2:

Buffett then asked the pilot to evaluate the list and circle his five most important goals. Once again, he took his time, went over the list, and marked his top 5 goals.

STEP 3:

By then, Flint had two lists. List A only contained the five circled items he had selected, and List B contained the 20 items he had not circled. At this point, the pilot smiled and stated that he would immediately start working on the list that included his five priorities,

"What about the second list?" Buffett asked him. *"What are you going to do with the options you did not circle?"*

"Well, those 20 are still important, they came in a close second, so I guess I'll have to work on them whenever I can. Although they are not as urgent, I still plan to spend some time on them."

"No! You've got it all wrong!" Buffett protested. *"Everything you did not circle just became your Avoid-At-All-Cost list! No matter what you do, you cannot*

afford to give them any time or attention until you've managed to succeed with your top 5!"

TIME EQUALS MONEY

Time is our most valuable resource. No matter who you are, rich or poor, you still only get 24 hours in a day. This is why time management is the most valued skill in the business and corporate industry. After all, time equals money.

Time and ideas are the one currency of the world we live in.

Think about it. We all get the same number of hours in a day, but somehow, few of us can make more out of it as compared to others. People keep thinking all the time how there is not enough time or if only they had more time. All these instances and examples only go to show how time is worth billions. It is abstract, but its effects are insuperable.

Time management is the phenomenon of inculcating and exercising the conscious usage of time in oneself by carefully allocating time to specific activities, which increase your productivity and efficiency and, thus, the odds of reaching success.

It means to plan, schedule, prioritize, and set goals to get specific things done in a set a time and thus optimize your habits to reach deadlines, eradicate procrastination, stress, and laziness from one's life.

Just think about it. If you don't have enough time to complete your work or are not able to deliver your tasks on time, then your professional life is bound to go down the gutter, even if all your priorities are in place.

IMPORTANCE OF TIME MANAGEMENT

The importance of time is hard to encompass. It is crucial, a finite resource like coal and oil. Everyone gets the same set of hours, but if treated wisely and assigned appropriately, you can make a whole set up from the ground up.

Although it does not have any monetary value attached to it, it can lead you to make serious bank. With adequate time management, you can achieve more with less work. If you breakdown a specific task in smaller chunks and assign timestamps to every single chunk which leads up to your deadline, you will be able to complete your work effectively and won't feel overworked in the least bit.

If you constantly feel like you are behind in submitting your work, in meeting deadlines, and keep missing out on opportunities, take control of your time right now. Don't let time run you; you should run it.

Time management also helps to add discipline to your life. Think about it. Even the world and nature around us follows a specific pattern and a particular timetable. The sun rises from the east at dawn, sets in the west at dusk. Birds chirp in the morning, and owls hoot at night.

Flowers bud in the spring and leaves fall from the trees in autumn. This entire set pattern happens according to a set time. They all are indirectly advising you to bring discipline and time management in your life.

The following are four vital habits you need to adopt when it comes to managing your time in the most efficient way:

1.-THE HABIT OF GETTING UP EARLY

Successful entrepreneurs know that getting up early is extremely important and that the first hours of the morning are always the most productive. Why?

Because in the morning our energy is freshest, our willpower highest and our mind and body less tired.

In his book *"Daily Rituals - How Artists Work,"* the Pennsylvania author, Mason Currey, analyzes the lives of some of the most prolific artists, thinkers, and achievers of all times, from Mozart to Voltaire, from Beethoven to Hemingway, from Benjamin Franklin to Vincent Van Gough. As Currey points out, most of these exceptional achievers were early risers and always did their most important work first. So, if you do not have the habit of getting up early, start making the necessary changes in your daily routine to develop it. It will definitely be worth it!

2.-THE HABIT OF PUNCTUALITY

When you become conscious of the usage of your time, you become punctual. It will set you on track for more victories, and you will be on the up and up in your career. This habit won't go unnoticed by your peers and colleagues, who will try to follow your example, talk about you, and praise you.

Your professional life will see a surge of achievements, whereas your personal life will also be stress-free; since you will no longer be lagging on projects. You will have more time for essential things; yourself, your family, and other relations. So how can you effectively manage your time?

3.-THE HABIT OF FOLLOWING A SCHEDULE

Time management directly correlates with how productive you are in a day. So, if you want to stay on top of things, plan your day every day. Make it a habit to keep a journal, set your daily goals, and organize them. Establish your priorities. Calculate how much time it may require you to complete a task. Make sure your timetable is effective yet flexible. Know when to cut it, remember that you don't need to overwork yourself to stay on top of your work.

4.-THE HABIT OF MINIMIZING DISTRACTIONS

Everyone would be able to manage their time more effectively if it weren't for distractions that keep steering us away from our life goals.

Distractions keep interrupting and disrupting your daily flow of life. For this, firstly, you need to exercise your focus. Whenever you feel your mind wandering away, bring it back. Drill it into your nature that your mind can't be carried away. Keep bringing yourself back every single time. Keep doing this until it becomes a natural habit.

To be able to focus relentlessly and undisturbed, you need to eradicate all distractions. This includes avoiding your phone, friends, unrelated activities, and anything else along those lines. Switch off your notifications, your mobiles, devices, and all the tabs on your browsers.

To get on top of your time management game, have time checks. Set time limits per task. Use alarms and other such technology. Join a support group. Delegate and outsource. Avoid perfection. Have a journal to plan always.

Also, avoid *"time wasters"* during the day. This includes not spending long periods on social media, watching Netflix, or sitting in front of a TV set. In fact, according to the American author Thomas Corley, who extensively studied the behavior of wealthy individuals before writing his revealing book *"Rich Habits,"* 67 percent watch TV for less than an hour a day. Instead, they spend their time engaged in self-improvement activities or working on their projects.

Of course, we are all susceptible to getting distracted when we have not allowed ourselves some time off. So, make sure you take out time for your well being too.

7.-THE HABIT OF PRIORITISING

"Relentless prioritization is about relentlessly asking ourselves what's essential to be completed today. And then focusing on what does have to be completed, which requires eliminating distractions—including random notifications, social media scrolling, and clearing low-priority emails."

Arianna Huffington

The greek-american entrepreneur and author Arianna Huffington, founder of The Huffington Post and CEO of Thrive Global, is one of the leading businesswomen in the United States. Included in Time Magazine's list of the world's 100 most influential people and the Forbes Most Powerful Women list, she believes one of the most critical working habits we need to develop if we aspire to succeed is what she calls *"relentless prioritization"*:

"When we're relentless in prioritizing what absolutely needs to be done, we're then able to accept the idea that other tasks and projects are not going to be completed today. This is important because it allows us to declare an end to the day, knowing that we've handed the essentials. And drawing that line between our day and our night allows us to let go of the day, which in turn allows us to go to sleep confident that we'll return to work tomorrow recharged and ready to take on that day's essential priorities."

Prioritizing tasks that need to be done vital for entrepreneurial growth and success. Not only personally, but it also constitutes a competitive advantage for companies that want to make use of the full potential of their employees and their business.

But, how should we prioritize our day to day work? And what determines which are the tasks that we first need to attend? According to the bestselling American writer Steven Pressfield, author of *"The War of Art,"* this should be done by wisely applying what he calls *"The Principle of Priority"*:

"The Principle of Priority states (a) you must know the difference between what is urgent and what is important, and (b) you must do what's important first."

Your priorities are the very difference between you reaching your full potential or you spending time doing nonsensical things and wasting your life away.

When you started reading these pages, you probably had some initial thoughts like, *"Man, I want to mend my ways and start focusing more on my work"* or perhaps, *"I spend all my time working but still can't reach my personal goals."* Well, as we have seen, this is not only because your past habits have been impeding it, but also because you probably do not have your priorities defined.

What is the one thing you want most in life? What are you willing to give in return? How important is it to you? And how much time do you spend on other things that are not as important?

If this is your case, then you probably don't have your priorities set in concrete. But, have no fear, for it's never too late to get on track by following the advice contained in these pages:

1.-Parse out your Priorities

The first thing you need to do is set your priorities. Start by listing your major ones, and then, your minor ones. After that, you need to determine which daily tasks or activities should be part of your top priorities.

Your major priorities can be making your business succeed, increasing your productivity, reducing your expenditures, working on a new project, developing a new skill, or improving your health, among others. Assign each a number from 1-10, depending on their importance. And do not let any guilt or other force drive you into making this decision.

This priority list needs to be truthful. To prioritize your tasks, you need to assign them a specific value. Which have the highest value, which are low order, and which are middle-order?

To determine these values, we can apply the classic system for prioritizing, known as the ABC system. Developed in 1970, it is based on the following three steps:

A.-FIRST STEP: Create an A-list with the tasks that need to be done first, including those that are overdue or with definite deadlines approaching soon. These are tasks for which there can be severe consequences if not completed. They are not necessarily the most important tasks that need to be done, but rather those that are already due or that soon will be.

For example, this may include preparing a report or presentation for a meeting, visiting a key customer, or paying specific bills. If you have more than one "A" task, you can prioritize these in your list by adding the labels A-1, A-2, A-3, and so on in front of each item.

B.-SECOND STEP: Now create a second list, or B list, including the tasks that are equally important, but less urgent (those that are not overdue or due soon). Usually, these are intermediate tasks that need to be done as a requisite for completing a superior task that may be done another day with little or no consequence.

This means that someone or something may be affected if you don't do these, but they are nowhere as important as an "A" task. For example, this may include returning an unimportant telephone call or text message or checking your email inbox. The rule of thumb is that you should never turn to a "B" task whenever there is an "A" task left undone.

C.-THIRD STEP: Finally, create the C list, including those tasks that are neither as essential nor due soon. These are particular tasks that can be pleasant and even fun to do, but of no consequence, if not done soon. For example, this may include phoning someone you know, having coffee or lunch with a friend or co-worker, or doing certain personal errands during work hours.

Applying the ABC Method to your to-do list helps you get organized and to complete the more important tasks first as well as faster.

D.-FOURTH STEP: Begin each day with a new ABC list and complete each task following the order of importance you have established. Keeping a daily ABC list will not only regulate your activities, but will also help you focus on what's more important, ensuring the perpetual success of your business. Therefore, start each day by setting your priorities according to the urgency and importance of each task.

Remember, one task may be important but not as important if you have another task overdue or due tomorrow. Also, if there is a task in your list that is very important, but does not require much time, skip it and concentrate on something that, if not completed today could certainly have immediate negative consequences, no matter how long this may take you.

Once you have figured out what to do in a day, decide on what to do first. There are two approaches to go about this. Some people start with easier tasks because completing them gives them a sense of victory and helps build momentum to complete bigger, more challenging projects. While some people start their day with the biggest tasks because you are most involved and vigorous at the start of the day as compared to the end of it.

Keep 4-5 daily goals every day and focus on them with the utmost vigilance. This will help you stay focused on what's most important. This is not just about minimizing distractions, suppressing the urge to scour Facebook or shopping online. It is about focusing on your top priorities.

Setting your daily goals will surely improve your productivity and help you get organized. It is the ultimate key action you need to take if you wish to get ahead.

Although you need to follow your top-priorities list, you also need to be flexible and adaptive in case something unexpected shows up. After all, you might have your day entirely scheduled and organized in an orderly fashion. But if something new shows up, and a new task that is equally urgent or important is suddenly thrown your way, you may need to change your priorities. So, make your list somewhat flexible to accommodate such situations, for we never know how our daily circumstances might change and how these will affect our list.

8.-THE HABIT OF TEAMWORK

"Teamwork is dependent on trusting the other folks to come through with their part without watching them all the time."

Steve Jobs

Although it is said that Steve Jobs occasionally lost his temper at work and would get angry with partners, employees, competitors, and even customers, it is a known fact that he was a great defender of teamwork and that all the companies he founded were incredibly collaborative.

Regarding Apple, he said the company was great at figuring out how to divide things up into great teams:

"There's tremendous teamwork at the top of the company, which filters down to tremendous teamwork throughout the company."

During a 1995 interview conducted by Bob Cringely for his PBS series *"Triumph of the Nerds,"* Jobs stressed the importance of teamwork in business and its undisputed effectiveness, mentioning one of his childhood episodes to depict how working together as a team can often produce great results.

According to Jobs, when he was a young kid, one of his neighbors was an old man in his eighties that lived up his street. Now, one day this man showed him a rare machine he had in his garage, known as a *"rock tumbler."* It consisted of a small electric motor with a small tin can attached to it.

Taking the can, he led the young boy to the back yard and told him to pick a few common and ugly rocks. After placing these inside the can, the man added a bit of fluid and grit powder before shutting the lid. After this, he attached the can to the motor, turned it on, and the can began to spin.

"Come back tomorrow," the old man told Jobs as the rocks, spinning within the can, began to make a lot of noise.

When Jobs returned the following day, the man turned off the motor, opened the can, and behold! One by one, he took out these incredibly attractive polished rocks. They did not look like the common rocks that had actually gone into the can. Then the man explained to him that their continuous friction had polished them, turning the rough stones into beautiful, polished gems, as Jobs explained:

"That's always been in my mind; it became my metaphor for a team working really hard on something they're passionate about. It's through the team, through that group of incredibly talented people, bumping up against each other, having arguments, having fights sometimes, making some noise, and working together, that they polish each other and polish their ideas. And what comes out are these really beautiful stones."

TEAMWORK MAKES THE DREAM WORK

When Bill Gates was asked about the main factor behind the success of Microsoft, he said it was teamwork, which can be defined as the art of managing a team to work together effectively, thus allowing its members to pull in the same direction and thus unlock their full potential.

Successful entrepreneurs know that teamwork produces nothing short of excellence. You might be a person with positive thinking, tactfully determined priorities, willing to take risks, and ready to grow, but if you don't know how to work with your team or never delegate, you are bound to fail.

It takes an army to run the corporate offices of Amazon, Google, Facebook, and more. But if you can't delegate your subordinates well, you will cause the whole empire to topple over. Teamwork is the skill that is most sought out by companies in their prospective candidates in job interviews.

A successful entrepreneur can never be a one-man-band. It simply does not work that way. Even Bill Gates was accompanied by his former friend, Paul Allen, when they created Microsoft. He could not have made it alone.

Remember the old saying:

"A champion team will defeat a team of champions."

And this statement holds a lot of substance. Let's unpack that:

IMPORTANCE OF TEAMWORK

Our society is quick to notice the smartest player in a team and lays more importance on him or her. However, the truth is that not always lone warriors can lead their team to victory. If that were the case, Stephen Curry would lead the Golden State Warriors to victory every single time.

Similarly, if Jeff Bezos, Elon Musk and Sir Richard Branson had not expanded their businesses and employed effective team-building strategies, their companies would have plummeted.

Although Walt Disney liked to draw and was actually good at it, he owed his success to his team. When he opened his first animation studio, he found partners who could make up for his personal limitations. One of his closest friends, Ub Iwerks, who was more talented, took the task of refining Mickey Mouse's image and was responsible for most of the early studio's animation. And it was Walt's brother Roy who actually ran the business and made it possible to finance Disney's big dreams.

When every single member of a team is valued and directed towards achieving one goal, an environment of unity is fostered. They all feel like a part of something bigger, something beyond themselves. They view their peers as their partners and work in unison with them to achieve their tasks. Thus, you need to foster such mentality in your subordinates and also join in on the spirit of teamwork and show loyalty to your co-workers.

In a team, all individuals may differ from each other in many, if not all, aspects. They usually have different perspectives, feedbacks, talents, skills, weaknesses, habits, and more. They may even clash if not united under one platform, but this individuality can also be benefitted off of.

Each individual can put forth their piece of mind, a different problem-solving strategy, individual creative ideas, and more. An effective team finds solutions more efficiently by brainstorming and sorting out issues collectively—output increases when everyone shares the input equally.

If we look at this from an evolutionary point of view, if our ancestors had not banded together, they would have never survived on their own.

Keep in mind that every member of a team is as diverse as he or she can get, possessing different talents and abilities. Therefore, they need to be aligned in such a way where they don't compete with each other to avoid an inefficient working environment, thus be able to work in harmony.

TEAMWORK AND SYNERGY

The term synergy comes from the Greek word *"synergos,"* meaning *"working together."* In modern organizational theory, however, synergy means much more than *"working together."*

Synergy refers to the benefit that results when two or more individual workers or teams combine efforts to achieve the same task and produce a greater outcome than what they would have each achieved on their own. It's the concept of the whole being greater than the sum of its parts. The potential for team synergy is defined by the combination of common interests, shared values, and complementary talents.

A basic assumption underlying the concept of synergy is that it can only be meaningful if there are at least two interacting resources.

In all cases, your role as a leader must be to facilitate the synergy between members of a specific team or between different management teams, with the object of generating an increased capacity and workflow that would not be possible when working independently. An effective synergy usually boosts employee creativity, competitivity, and efficiency, generating more efficacy and higher profitability.

Although synergy is often associated with positive outcomes (for example, the creation of synergistic knowledge within a group, which is beyond the knowledge initially held by the individual members of the team), negative synergy may also occur when one resource degrades the effect of another leading to less beneficial outcomes.

Among other benefits of synergistic teamwork is that individuals learn to support each other, encourage each other, motivate each other, tackle problems together, their productivity and efficiency increase, you can get a year's work done in a day; all this cooperation promotes workplace synergy.

It also helps to discard all errors since you learn from those around you. Your skillset starts to expand.

Those around you multiply your vision. One's mistake can be covered by another's success.

MAIN PROBLEMS OF TEAMWORK

According to the *Harvard Business Review*, there are eight main problems that we need to avoid when working in teams:

1.-Absence of team identity. This occurs when the members of a team do not feel reciprocally responsible for reaching the team's objectives or suffer from a lack of commitment and effort, usually generating conflict or poor collaboration among them.

2.-Difficulty making decisions. This takes place when team members are inflexible in their points of view, refuse to change their arguments, or reject new ones without evaluating them.

3.-Poor communication. This is when members of a team interrupt, talk over one another, or remain silent in meetings, often reaching consensus without a real agreement.

4.-Inability to solve conflicts. This is when inner tensions or personal attacks among team members do not allow them to solve conflicts or reach consensus.

5.-Lack of participation. This is due to poor attendance or low energy during meetings, causing poor participation among team members, who, therefore, cannot complete their tasks and assignments.

6.-Lack of creativity. This is generated by poor individual perspectives and lack of ideas, impeding team members from developing creative solutions, or taking advantage of new opportunities.

7.-Groupthink. This is when strong team agreements make its members show no critical thinking or willingness to debate and cannot adopt fresh alternatives or approaches.

8.-Ineffective leadership. This is caused by the absence of a leader with a unitary group vision, preventing team members from unifying their different points of view and priorities.

9.-THE HABIT OF LEARNING FROM FAILURE

"Many of life's failures are people who did not realize how close they were to success when they gave up."

Thomas A. Edison

One of Thomas Alva Edison's first patented inventions was the *"the electrographic vote-recorder,"* which he proposed to the US Senate as a mechanism to increase accuracy and *"save several hours of public time every day in the session."* Although it was a great invention, it was soundly rejected by the political leaders of his time because they feared it would hurt the usual vote trading and maneuvering among senators, and end up subverting the entire legislative process.

Despite his rotund disappointment, Edison took his failure in stride and, from that point on, as the American historian Leonard Degraaf informs, *"he vowed he would not invent a technology that didn't have an apparent market; that he wasn't just going to invent things for the sake of inventing them but...to be able to sell them. I have to suspect that even Edison, as a young and inexperienced innovator at that point, would have had to understand that if he can't sell his invention, he can't make money."*

So, after all, thanks to his failure, Edison managed to learn a most valuable lesson, paving the way for his many "commercial" inventions.

Regarding his electric lamp or incandescent light bulb, Edison admitted that when he was working on it, he tried 10,000 different fibers before settling on the carbon filament. And when one of his assistants mentioned these failures, he said:

"No, they were not failures. They taught me something that I didn't know. They taught me what not to do and which direction to move in."

LEARN FROM YOUR FAILURES

Seasoned entrepreneurs know that each time we fail, there is always something to learn from and grow as individuals. Failure makes you stronger, resistant, and persistent.

Abraham Lincoln lost eight elections and had two failed businesses before becoming one of the greatest presidents in America.

Henry Ford went bankrupt three times before succeeding. And, before he became one of the most renowned entrepreneurs in history, he failed at finding solid financial backing for the production of his first motor vehicle.

Nonetheless, he learned from his own failure and ultimately found the way to succeed, not only changing the world's automobile industry forever but also creating an innovative manufacturing process capable of producing low-cost, reliable products: the world's first moving assembly line.

"Success," said IBM founder T. J. Watson, *"is on the far side of failure."*

When starting out a new project, try to keep in mind that you will probably mess up. You will make mistakes. You will have faults. You will have flaws. And thus, you will probably fail. But that is okay, for making mistakes is the first step to learning and improving.

But also keep in mind that your flops are nothing but an opportunity to learn and grow, to innovate and improve. Even Coca-Cola, which presently generates revenue in billions, only earned 200 dollars in its first year of business.

As Sir Richard Branson says:

"You don't learn to walk by following rules. You learn by doing, and by falling over."

If you never make mistakes, you will never know what you lack and need to work on. You will never become a better version of yourself. You will be stuck in your ways of going about things unless you learn from your mistakes.

Letting your mistakes bog you down is a negative habit. So, in the face of mistakes and hardships, try to maintain a positive outlook.

This is a wonderful way to assess your mistakes. Because you might be defeated now, but at least you now know what does not work. And this certainly gives you a head start. Therefore, if you make a mistake, do not beat yourself about it. Work on it. Identify where you went wrong, why you did, and what needs fixing. Begin from scratch once again and keep trying, even if you have to start over a zillion times.

In sum, do not disregard your mistakes or shove them under the carpet. Embrace them. The first step to learning from your mistakes is embracing them. And, once you nullify all your mistakes, the only way left will be onwards and upwards. After all, as Napoleon Hill expressed:

"Every failure brings with it the seed of an equivalent success."

When Elon Musk created SpaceX, he faced repeated failures and lost large sums of money. In fact, he came close to bankruptcy. But finally, SpaceX achieved its first effective launch and subsequently earned a $1.6 billion contract from NASA. Instead of giving up, Musk chose to keep fighting for his dream until the last moment and was duly rewarded for his determination and perseverance.

Be positive. Do not give up. Learn from each failure, and always be optimistic when times go wrong, like Edison, who is also known for saying that *"our greatest weakness lies in giving up. The most certain way to succeed is always to try just one more time."*

10.-A FINAL WORD OF ADVICE

According to the *Global Entrepreneurship Monitor,* over 582 million entrepreneurs are presently in the process of starting up or running their own company. However, a staggering 50% of all new start-ups fail within the first five years, and 8 out of 10 fail within the first year.

In order to succeed, as we have seen, you will definitely need to develop winning habits and to develop these, you need to change your mindset.

We all know that life has its ups and downs. One moment it can be joyful and pleasant, and the other can be full of obstacles and distress. However, if you develop positive habits, you can quickly recover and be productive even on your worst days.

If, for example, you've experienced specific problems in the morning and cannot focus correctly, your good habits can help you make the most of the rest of your day, regardless of any trouble you may have experienced.

Now that we know how important our habits are and how they govern every sphere of our lives, we can begin to understand the immense, immaculate importance of cultivating and following up on good habits. We know that for most people, this must be a daunting thought. Change is not easy. It certainly does not come by with the snap of fingers. It is not magic.

To change your bad habits, you need to want to change yourself and your daily life patterns. You have to actively block out your negative traits and replace them with productive routine actions able to support you and your ambitions.

Change may be hard to come about but not impossible. My advice is to take small steps every day to replace one bad habit with one good habit.

Usually, once you are done with a toxic habit, your brain releases certain chemicals that give you a feeling of well-being. Therefore, if you are planning to replace a bad habit with a good one, make sure the better habit also provides the same rewards.

Habits take around 3-4 weeks to change. In this process, be consistent with yourself. Be there to pick yourself up if you falter. Appreciate yourself for all the small efforts that you make along the way. Join a support group of people who are trying to adopt similar smart habits and people whose ambitions are alike yours.

You will feel motivated to make progress and find solace in your defeats. Change your today for a better tomorrow and remember: In the end, the only real success is having successful habits.

Now go out there and change the world!

A. J. Parr

ENTREPRENEUR MINDSET SERIES

By A.J. Parr

VOL 1

*The Ten Golden Rules of Entrepreneurial Success
and Financial Wealth*

VOL 2

Top Habits of Successful Entrepreneurs

VOL 3

Emotional Intelligence for Entrepreneurs

ALL RIGHTS RESERVED – FAIR USE

All Rights Reserved under Title 17, U.S. Code, International, and Pan-American Copyright Conventions. The sharing, duplication, distribution, uploading, or transfer of this electronic book by any digital or printed means without the explicit permission of the publisher is unauthorized.

DISCLAIMER: The 1976 Copyright Act (Section 107) states that "fair use" is permitted when writing criticism, comments, news reports, and didactic texts (otherwise infringing). Non-profit, educational, or personal use favor fair use. Napoleon Hill quotes taken from the 1937 edition of "Think and Grow Rich" presently in the Public Domain

AUTHOR: A.J. Parr

PUBLISHED BY: Grapevine Books

ediciones delaparra@gmail.com

GRAPEVINE BOOKS

FIRST EDITION 2020

Copyright © 2020 A. J. Parr. All Rights Reserved

www.ingramcontent.com/pod-product-compliance
Lightning Source LLC
Chambersburg PA
CBHW070409220526
45467CB00001B/514